First
Facts

T0100960

Thomas Edison

PHYSICIST AND INVENTOR

by Mary Boone

CAPSTONE PRESS
a capstone imprint

First Facts are published by Capstone Press,
1710 Roe Crest Drive, North Mankato, Minnesota 56003
www.mycapstone.com

Library of Congress Cataloging-in-Publication Data:
Library of Congress Cataloging-in-Publication Data is available on the Library of
Congress website.

ISBN: 978-1-5435-0647-1 (library binding) -- 978-1-5435-0653-2 (paperback) --
978-1-5435-0659-4 (ebook)

Summary: This book presents the life of Thomas Edison, the physicist who invented the
phonograph, Kinetograph, and safe lightbulb.

Editorial Credits
Anna Butzer, editor; Bobbie Nuytten, designer;
Jo Miller, media researcher; Laura Manthe, production specialist

Photo Credits
Getty Images: Corbis Historical/Library of Congress, 21, The LIFE Picture Collection/
David E. Scherman, 11; Library of Congress, 7; Newscom: Documenta/Album, 9,
Mondadori Portfolio, 13, The Print Collector Heritage Images, 15, World History Archive,
17; Shutterstock: Everett Historical, cover (portrait), 5, 17 (inset), Marzolino, cover
(lightbulb); The Image Works: Topham, 19

Design Elements
Shutterstock: SeDmi

Printed in the United States of America.
010868S18

Table of Contents

CHAPTER 1

Young Edison

Have you ever turned on a light or watched a video? If so, your life has been touched by the **genius** of Thomas Alva Edison. He invented things we still use today. His inventions have changed over time. Thomas Edison's ideas are still seen almost everywhere.

genius—remarkable talent or intelligence

Thomas in his West Orange, New Jersey, laboratory, 1901

Thomas was born February 11, 1847, in Milan, Ohio. When he was 12, he started selling newspapers and snacks on a train. As a teen he saved a toddler from a runaway train. The child's father thanked Thomas by teaching him to use a **telegraph**. This sparked Thomas' interest in **communications**.

Homeschooled

Thomas did not do well in school. He asked a lot of questions. This annoyed his teacher. The teacher said Thomas' brains were "addled" or scrambled. This angered Thomas' mother. She decided to teach him at home. Years later Thomas said that his mother "was the most enthusiastic champion a boy ever had."

telegraph—a machine that uses electronic signals to send messages over long distances

communications—the ways of sending information to people

Thomas at age 14

CHAPTER 2

Curiosity Leads to Invention

Thomas started working as a telegraph operator when he was 15. In his spare time, he enjoyed taking things apart to see how they worked. His curiosity led him to **patent** his first invention when he was 20 — a vote counting machine. The machine worked, but it never caught on.

patent—a legal document giving an inventor sole rights to make and sell an item he or she invented

In 1869 Thomas moved to New York. He started an **engineering** company. In 1871 he invented a machine that printed **stock** prices. The Gold and Stock Telegraph Company bought the machine for $40,000. It was a lot of money at the time. Thomas had sold his first invention.

engineering—using science to design and build things

stock—a share of a company that can be bought, sold, or traded

close-up of the stock ticket printing machine Thomas invented

GOLD & STOCK TELEGRAPH Co.
UNIVERSAL PRINTER
EDISON'S PATENT
Nº 215

CHAPTER 3

The Most Famous Inventions

Thomas invented thousands of things during his life. He may be best known for the light bulb. However, he did not invent the first light bulb. He did develop the first light bulb that could safely be used in a home. He also invented switches that easily turned lights on and off.

FACT Before the light bulb, people burned candles or lamp oil. Electric lights were safer and easier to use.

Thomas holding a light bulb in his laboratory in Menlo Park, New Jersey, 1910

Thomas knew a lot about the telegraph. This knowledge helped him invent the phonograph. The phonograph recorded and played back sound. It used needles and tin-covered **cylinders**. Thomas spent 52 years on this invention. The phonograph was patented in 1878.

"I always invented to obtain money to go on inventing."

Thomas Edison

cylinder—a shape with flat, circular ends and sides shaped like a tube

Thomas with his phonograph, 1878

Thomas and his employee W. K. L. Dickson invented a movie camera called the Strip Kinetograph. They also invented a way to watch the movies by looking through a **peephole** viewer. They called it the Kinetoscope. In 1893 Thomas built a movie studio. The studio made almost 1,200 short films.

Hearing Impairment

A childhood illness caused Thomas to lose most of his hearing. People asked him why he didn't invent a hearing aid. He often said he was working on one. But Thomas thought that being deaf helped him. He wasn't distracted from his work.

peephole—a small opening through which you can look

man looks into a Kinetoscope, invented in 1889

CHAPTER 4

More Inventions

Thomas was an excellent **physicist** and is known as one of the greatest inventors in the world. However, not all of Thomas' inventions were successful. Sometimes his ideas just didn't sell. One of these inventions was an electric pen. Other times it took a long time to get an invention right. He said it took him 1,000 tries to make a light bulb that worked.

"I have not failed. I've just found 10,000 ways that won't work."

Thomas Edison

physicist—scientist who studies physics

Mina and Thomas in his laboratory, 1906

Family History

Edison was married twice. He married Mary Stilwell in 1871. They had three children. Mary died in 1884. He married Mina Miller in 1886. He had three more children with her.

Even late in life, Thomas kept inventing. In 1912 automaker Henry Ford asked Thomas to design a battery for the **Model T**. Thomas also invented an electric lamp for miners and a machine to view X-rays. Thomas died October 18, 1931, in West Orange, New Jersey. He was 94 years old.

FACT The Thomas Edison National Historical Park is in West Orange, New Jersey. Visitors can tour Edison's laboratories, libraries, and home.

Model T—an early type of automobile made by the Ford Motor Company in 1908

Henry Ford (left) and Thomas Edison, 1915

Glossary

communications (kuh-myoo-nuh-KAY-shuhnz)—the ways of sending information to people

cylinder (SI-luhn-duhr)—a shape with flat, circular ends and sides shaped like a tube

engineering (en-juh-NEER-ing)—using science to design and build things

genius (JEE-nee-uhss)—remarkable talent or intelligence

Model T (MOD-uhl TEE)—an early type of automobile made by the Ford Motor Company in 1908

patent (PAT-uhnt)—a legal document giving an inventor sole rights to make and sell an item he or she invented

peephole (PEEP-hohl)—a small opening through which you can look

physicist (FIZ-uh-sist)—scientist who studies physics

stock (STOK)—a share of a company that can be bought, sold, or traded

telegraph (TEL-uh-graf)—a machine that uses electronic signals to send messages over long distances

Read More

Barnham, Kay. *Thomas Edison*. Science Biographies. Chicago: Raintree, 2014.

Jones, Charlotte Foltz. *Mistakes that Worked: The World's Familiar Inventions and How They Came to Be*. New York: Delacorte Press, 2015.

Miller, Rachel, Holly Homer, and Jamie Harrington. *The 101 Coolest Simple Science Experiments*. Salem, Mass.: Page Street Publishing, 2016.

Sandler, Martin W. *Inventors*. A Library of Congress Book. New York: HarperCollins, reprinted 2014.

Internet Sites

Use FactHound to find Internet sites related to this book.

Visit *www.facthound.com*

Just type in 9781543506471 and go!

Check out projects, games and lots more at
www.capstonekids.com

Critical Thinking Questions

1. How do you think light bulbs have changed since Thomas Edison's day?

2. Thomas was good at marketing his inventions. Pretend you are Thomas in the 1890s. How would you advertise your new movie camera and viewer?

3. Would Thomas have been as successful as he was if he lived today? Why or why not?

Index